WHAT

MILLy

THE REMARKABLE

DID

PIONEER OF PLASTICS RECYCLING

Elise Moser

PICTURES BY
SCOT RITCHIE

GROUNDWOOD BOOKS
HOUSE OF ANANSI PRESS
TORONTO   BERKELEY

The publisher would like to thank Joseph Van Rossum, Natural
Resources Educator at University of Wisconsin-Extension, for
checking the text.

Groundwood Books / House of Anansi Press
groundwoodbooks.com

We acknowledge for their financial support of our publishing
program the Canada Council for the Arts, the Ontario Arts Council
and the Government of Canada.

Canada Council
for the Arts

Conseil des Arts
du Canada

ONTARIO ARTS COUNCIL
CONSEIL DES ARTS DE L'ONTARIO
an Ontario government agency
un organisme du gouvernement de l'Ontario

With the participation of the Government of Canada
Avec la participation du gouvernement du Canada | Canadä

Groundwood Books is
committed to protecting our
natural environment. This
book was printed at Friesens,
which operates hydro-powered
plants that produce no air
pollutants, no toxic waste and
contribute 18-60 times fewer
greenhouse gases than natural
gas or coal-fired plants. It was
printed on a UV web press
that emits no Volatile Organic
Compounds. The interior
of this book was printed
with vegetable-based inks
on paper that contains 100%
post-consumer recycled fibers,
is acid-free and is processed
chlorine-free.

MIX
Paper from
responsible sources
FSC® C016245
www.fsc.org

Library and Archives Canada Cataloguing in Publication
Moser, Elise, author
What Milly did : the remarkable pioneer of plastics recycling / Elise
Moser ; pictures by Scot Ritchie.
Issued in print and electronic formats.
ISBN 978-1-55498-994-2 (hardback). — ISBN 978-1-55498-893-8
(paperback). — ISBN 978-1-55498-894-5 (html).
— ISBN 978-1-55498-895-2 (mobi)
1. Zantow, Milly — Juvenile literature. 2. Recycling (Waste, etc.) —
Juvenile literature. 3. Green movement — Juvenile literature.
4. Environmentalism — Juvenile literature.
I. Ritchie, Scot, illustrator
II. Title.
TD794.5.M68 2016   j363.72'82   C2015-908452-0
C2015-908453-9

Cover illustration by Scot Ritchie
The illustrations were done in ink and Photoshop.
Design by Michael Solomon
Printed and bound in Canada

To everyone who makes the world better with creativity, determination and hard work — especially those of you who may never be recognized for your efforts. This is for you, with love.

WHAT MILLY DID

Milly Zantow Changed the World

You've probably never heard of her. She wasn't a superstar or a princess. She didn't invent lifesaving medicines, or the internet, or candy that fizzes inside your mouth. But she did create something you probably see every day. And because of her, there's a lot less plastic garbage in the world.

Milly was born on an Oklahoma farm in 1923 — almost a hundred years ago! There were seven kids in her family, living with their parents in a small house with only four rooms. As soon as Milly was old enough to talk she went to live with her grandmother, who lived in her own little house on the farm. There, as a small child, Milly started working.

Milly's grandmother kept a loom in the kitchen (the warmest room in the house), and she would weave rugs, likely from strips of old clothing, while Milly sat on a little stool tending the warp strings so they didn't snag. While they worked together, Milly's grandma sang to her or told her stories.

At that time people reused everything they could because they had to. There was no recycling as it exists now, but people found new uses for all sorts of things at home.

Recycling Now — and Then

These days most of us take recycling for granted. We sort our garbage, recycling and compost at home (unless we keep the compost for our own lawns and gardens). We know the recycled stuff will be made into new objects of all kinds.

Your old homework might become your next birthday card. An empty olive oil bottle can be recycled into an olive jar or beautiful tiles for the kitchen. Recycled glass is sometimes mixed into road-paving materials. Aluminum from a soft drink can might be made into new aluminum cans, aluminum foil or building materials. Plastics will find new life as drainage pipes, carpeting or recycled fabrics (your cozy fleece jacket might be made from pop bottles).

It seems obvious that we should reuse our metals, glass and plastics by recycling them — after all, these are non-renewable materials. That means their supply is limited. They come out of the earth — metal from ore, glass from sand, and plastics from oil — and once we use up what was created long ago

RECYCLED BRIDGE

There is a bridge in Scotland made of recycled plastic bottles and plastic household waste. It's strong enough to carry forty-four tons of pedestrians, cars and trucks. Not only that, it won't ever rust or need to be painted. And when it finally has to be removed, many years from now, it can simply be — can you guess? — recycled!

(maybe even when our planet was formed) it will be gone.

We should recycle paper too, even though it's a renewable resource. It is most often made from trees, but it takes a long time to grow trees — plus a lot of energy (electricity, gasoline and human labor) to harvest and transport them, then process them in the paper mill. Even better, paper is easy to recycle.

It may be hard to imagine that just thirty or forty years ago, probably around the time your parents were born, most people just tossed *everything* in the trash — pop cans, juice bottles, newspapers, plastic milk jugs and cat food cans. When the garbage trucks came around, they squished everything together into a big stinky pile and drove to a big hole in the ground called a landfill. There, they simply dumped it all out.

What a waste!

How It All Began

In 1978, Milly Zantow was working as a
volunteer for the International Crane Foundation, a bird conservation group near her
home in the Baraboo Hills of southern Wisconsin. She went on a trip to Tokyo to rep-
resent the foundation at a meeting with the
Japanese emperor. Cranes are very important
symbols in Japanese culture, representing
happiness and luck.

While she was in Japan, Milly noticed
that when she came out onto the street each
morning, people had placed little bundles at
the curb. Every day it was something different. One day it was glass, another day paper,
another day metal. Soon Milly understood
that the Japanese were separating their waste
and putting it out for recycling. Japan is a
very small country with a lot of people living
in it, and they didn't have enough space to
dump everything in landfills the way North
Americans were used to doing. She was impressed with how clean everything was. The
idea of recycling made sense to her.

Shortly after she got home, Milly heard

that her local landfill was almost full. Not only that, poisons were leaking into the underground water supply, which was bad for people and the environment. The county was building a new landfill, but some people worried that it wouldn't be ready in time — in fact, it might take as long as three years. Imagine all the garbage that could pile up in

THE INTERNATIONAL CRANE FOUNDATION

Milly saw recycling in action when she went to Japan as a volunteer for the International Crane Foundation (ICF).

The ICF runs conservation programs as far away as Siberia and Mongolia. Some of their most successful programs help cranes by finding ways for them to live in harmony with humans.

You can visit the ICF in Wisconsin and walk on environmentally friendly recycled-glass walkways through a restored prairie landscape. It's the only place where you can see all of the world's crane species. If you're lucky, you'll see whooping cranes "dance." "Whoopers" were almost extinct in the 1940s, but today there are hundreds.

Your family or your class at school can adopt a crane at the ICF. Visit www.savingcranes.org.

three years! Milly decided to find out what exactly was filling up that landfill.

One morning she got up and went out to the garbage dump. She climbed to the top of the pile and sat there all day. She counted the trucks that came in and watched what they were dumping. She noticed that there was a lot of plastic — all kinds of plastic. This was not good news, because Milly knew that mountain of plastic would stay there for a very long time.

A Garbage Crisis

Milly wasn't the only one worried about how fast the waste was accumulating in her local landfill. Sauk County wasn't the only place with too much trash and nowhere to put it. In fact, some people were saying that there was a "garbage crisis."

Why?

One reason was simply that the population was increasing. But also, since World War II, which ended in 1945, people's habits had changed. They were generating more garbage than they used to. For example, in a lot of places, soft drinks were sold in refillable glass bottles until the 1960s. But when soda companies switched to non-refillable cans, the cans all ended up in the trash. Plus, products came in more packaging than before. Instead of carrying apples home from the store in a reusable bag, people bought plastic bags of apples and carried them home in another plastic bag. Then they threw out all the bags.

Plastics, which only became common in products and packaging in the late 1940s, became a big part of our garbage in just a few decades.

Milly knew that some garbage breaks down quickly, like apple cores or toast crumbs from your breakfast. That kind of

MORE ABOUT PLASTICS

We use plastics every day, from sandwich wrap to medical supplies, computer parts, even your toothbrush. Produced as part of the oil-refining process, most plastics have only existed since the 1950s.

Because plastics take so long to break down, recycling is important to save landfill space. But we also need to conserve our supply of plastic since petroleum, the oil most plastics are made of, is a non-renewable resource.

Our plastic garbage can cause serious problems for sea and land animals. Sometimes they eat it by mistake, or become tangled in it. Some plastics get worn down into tiny bits and pollute the oceans. New research says that little balls of plastic called microbeads (often used to make the scrubby bits in toothpaste) and tiny recycled plastic fibers from our clothing are polluting our waters, including the oceans and the Great Lakes. Some plastics give off poisons into the water and air.

To solve these problems, scientists are working on making plastics from plants, or finding bacteria or fungi that can digest plastics made from oil. But for now, recycling is the best choice.

plant-based stuff, along with the leaves you rake in the fall or grass cuttings from mowing the lawn, can be composted. It rots and quickly becomes rich new soil. That's very valuable. We put it back on the lawn or in the garden, where the roots of the plants can get the nutrients and minerals they need to grow big and healthy.

But unlike plant matter, plastics usually take several lifetimes — sometimes as long as a thousand years — to break down. Remembering what she'd seen in Japan, Milly suspected that these piles of plastic waste that were being dumped and buried could be recycled instead, freeing up the land that was being used for dumping, and helping solve the landfill problem. She suggested this solution to the county board. But they told her nobody was recycling plastics — nobody had figured out how.

Milly Figures It Out

Milly knew a practical method of recycling plastics had to be possible. But she also knew that even if she showed people how to do it, they wouldn't bother unless they saw why it was important.

During World War II, when Milly was a young woman, resources were scarce because they were reserved for the war effort — for making things like uniforms, airplanes and ammunition. Some food and other goods were in short supply. Ordinary people did their part by recycling. Volunteers, for example women's groups and Boy Scouts, collected materials like scrap metal, rubber from old tires, and paper.

But once the war was over, they stopped. Recycling reminded them of what it was like to struggle with shortages. They associated repairing and reusing things with being poor. By 1978, when Milly faced her garbage dump full of plastic, wartime recycling was so far in the past that a lot of people didn't even know it had ever been done. She had to start from scratch to convince people that recycling was important — this time to save the environment.

Milly also knew that folks would like it if they could save money — or make money — by recycling. This was true for families recycling plastic milk jugs or shampoo bottles at home, and also for entire communities managing their waste.

Milly realized that it wasn't enough to collect all the plastic. She had to have a plan for what to do with it afterward. She was a creative and determined person. Step by step, she designed a whole system to make plastics recycling possible.

How Did She Do It?

Milly started by teaching herself all about the different plastics and why they weren't already being recycled. She read a plastics encyclopedia. She talked to plastics experts. She called the Borden Dairy Company in Milwaukee and asked them how they manufactured their plastic milk jugs. What did they do when they made a mistake? she asked. They told her they just melted the deformed jug down and reblew it.

That was an "Aha!" moment for Milly. If they could melt down and reblow the milk jugs during the manufacturing process, they could recycle them after they'd been used too.

She approached Flambeau Plastics, located near her home in Baraboo. She knew the Sauey family, who owned the company. She asked them to help her figure out how to use recycled plastic to make some of their products.

Originally founded to make frog-shaped plastic fishing lures, Flambeau now made all kinds of plastic products, including the famous Duncan yo-yos. They told Milly that

DUNCAN YO-YOS

Yo-yos are among the oldest toys in history, invented thousands of years ago, probably in China or ancient Greece.

A Filipino immigrant, Pedro Flores, brought the idea for this toy to California, where Donald F. Duncan first saw one in 1928. Flambeau Plastics started making them in 1969.

Yo-yos are popular the world over — and beyond. A yellow one went into outer space on the space shuttle *Discovery*!

recycling wasn't practical because there were more than seven types of plastic and they couldn't be melted together. Nobody had invented a way of separating the different forms of plastic.

Milly didn't let that stop her. She went to the University of Wisconsin campus in Baraboo ("Boo U") and learned how to use different types of tests to identify the various plastics. There were burn tests, smoke tests, a water-weight test and a scratch test. Some of the tests were dangerous, but Milly learned how to do them so she could separate the plastics for recycling.

Flambeau agreed to experiment to see what new products they could make out of recycled plastic. But there was a hitch — the plastic had to be ground up before they could melt it down.

Milly did more research. She found a company in Chicago that made industrial plastic grinders. She asked them to sell her one. They laughed at her. They weren't used to having white-haired women come along and buy their big industrial machines, and they had never heard of anyone trying to recycle household plastic waste. But Milly convinced them she was serious, and they finally agreed. The machine would cost five thousand dollars.

Milly didn't have an extra five thousand dollars. She didn't know what to do.

One evening, her friend Jenny Ehl came over. Milly told Jenny her idea. They decided to cash in their life insurance policies to get the five thousand dollars. Milly figured she didn't need that life insurance money right away, but they did need that machine.

Cash in hand, Milly and Jenny climbed into a pickup truck and drove to Chicago to buy their grinder. The men at the company "just died laughing when they saw us," Milly said. But Milly and Jenny didn't let that bother them. They loaded the heavy grinder into their truck — "It weighed a ton!" said Milly — and drove it back to Wisconsin.

"Waste isn't waste until it's wasted..."

In 1979, with their grinder set up in a nearby warehouse, Milly and Jenny founded E-Z Recycling.

Milly and Jenny didn't start their company with the idea of making a lot of money for themselves. Their goal was to do something useful for the community. They wanted to educate people about the benefits of recycling. Milly had seen all the different things that were being recycled in Japan, so she knew that too much valuable stuff was being buried in garbage dumps in North America. Plastics, metals, paper — even motor oil — all kinds of things could be used again or made into something new. "It's a sin to bury money," Milly and Jenny said.

But it wasn't only about money — it was about waste. Milly told her local newspaper that it made her "heartsick" to see the landfill full of things that could have been reused.

Maybe Milly was remembering her childhood.

Back on the farm, they didn't have money

to spend. In those days credit cards didn't exist — cash was the only money. The only cash income for Milly's whole family came from selling their cows' cream, which meant they had to produce almost everything they needed. They grew a lot of their own food. Milly's grandmother made bread for the large family every single day, baking it in a wood-burning oven. They kept chickens, and in the winter it was little Milly who had to collect the eggs from the henhouse before they froze.

Milly's family fixed anything that broke instead of throwing it away, because they couldn't afford to buy anything new. When her dad's overalls were so worn out that they couldn't be mended anymore, Milly's mom found a few spots that were still whole to make mittens for the girls. Can you imagine going to school wearing mittens sewn from your dad's old overalls?

After living through that as a child, no wonder Milly was troubled when she saw piles of useful objects or reusable materials in the garbage.

Milly and Jenny imagined what it meant

to have tons of trash piling up all over the planet. They guessed that nearly 40 percent of the garbage going to their local landfill was paper and cardboard, which could easily be recycled if someone collected and processed it.

We often have the idea that paper falls apart easily, but it can last for years buried in a landfill. If you went to a garbage dump and dug up a newspaper that was published the day you were born, you might still be able to open it up and read it. That's because paper can't break down unless it is exposed to the air and rain, or composted, or processed in a recycling plant. Milly used to say, "Waste isn't waste until it's wasted."

"You have to start with the people..."

Milly and Jenny knew that some newspaper was being recycled in their community, but no one was recycling plastic. So they convinced the students and teachers at Spruce Street School and St. Aloysius School in Sauk City, close to E-Z Recycling's warehouse, to collect plastic containers.

Not everybody was happy about this strange new activity. Milly laughed when, years later, she told a visitor about getting angry phone calls from local moms — they didn't like their kids dragging in junk they picked up on the walk home from school. The idea of recycling was still so new, those moms couldn't imagine that the dirty old plastic their kids found in the gutter was anything but trash. It would be much more, though, when Milly and Jenny got through with it.

Near the end of the school year they went to pick up all the recyclables the kids had collected. They were so impressed with the kids' efforts that they wrote a letter to the local newspaper congratulating the two schools for helping them make a success of their new recycling plan.

"We hope you'll continue recycling during

THE *PLASTIKI*

When David de Rothschild read that our deep oceans contained more than 70 million pounds (31 million kilograms) of plastic garbage, he decided to encourage people to change their plastic habits. In 2010, he and his team built an entire boat out of recycled garbage and sailed it across the Pacific Ocean from San Francisco to Sydney, Australia.

They used 12,500 recycled plastic bottles filled with air to make the hulls. The mast was made from a reused aluminum irrigation pipe, and the sails from post-consumer PET plastic. They even created their own environmentally friendly glue out of cashew nuts and sugar. Mmmm, delicious!

The plastic items they found most frequently in the ocean were plastic bottles, Styrofoam cups, lids from soda and water bottles, and plastic bags.

summer vacation," they said, "and for as long as we need to recycle to help save our natural resources."

That was in 1980 — a long time ago! But we still need to recycle to help save our natural resources, now more than ever.

Because the goal of their business wasn't to make a profit, Milly and Jenny made some unusual choices that helped them get their company going while doing good in the community. For example, in Sauk City they decided not to collect aluminum cans because the students at St. Aloysius were already doing that (using the money they raised, the kids bought a new microscope for the school). Milly and Jenny chose not to accept newspapers because the Boy Scouts were collecting those.

They also offered to help nearby towns establish their own recycling programs if they didn't want to bring their recycling to E-Z. It was more important to Milly and Jenny to see recycling take place than to get the business for themselves.

They also decided to hire people who might have a hard time getting a job somewhere else, and help prepare them to find better jobs later. They hired moms on welfare, people who had been in prison and people with developmental disabilities.

"That was a great source of pride for those workers," says Liz Nevers, who was a volunteer at E-Z Recycling. "We said you have to start with the people."

She was inspired by the experience to go back to school and get an MA degree in Solid Waste and Recycling, which she calls a "master's in garbage."

Six Days a Week

By the end of that first summer Milly and
her team were collecting a variety of plastics,
paper, rags, glass and metals, and they had a
collection point in a nearby town where folks
could drop off their recyclable materials.
Eventually they would have collection points
in seven towns in their area.

Milly and Jenny worked six days a week.
"And then if we had a good March wind, it
was seven days a week, 'cause I chased the
stuff all the way up the highway as it blew
away," Milly said. They separated recyclables,
sorted paper and cardboard, and crushed
aluminum cans from towns where there was
no competition from school kids.

Milly and Jenny worked really hard processing all the recycling. At the beginning,
they washed and dried and cleaned the labels
off thousands of plastic milk jugs. Flambeau
Plastics didn't want to get a few pounds of
plastic at a time — in fact, they didn't want
less than 10,000 pounds (4,535 kilograms)
in each delivery. There were seven jugs per
pound, so Milly and Jenny and their vol-

unteer helpers had to wash, dry and grind 70,000 milk jugs for every load! They also smashed every glass jar and crushed every tin can with a sledgehammer. Sometimes Milly had to get up at 4 a.m. on Saturday mornings to see to the loading of 900-pound (408-kilogram) bales of paper and cardboard into semi-trailers. Imagine that!

Milly put her body on the line. She got frostbite on her feet from working in the unheated warehouse in the winter. She was hurt using the cardboard baler, and she cut her hands on broken glass. But she wasn't working alone — she inspired other folks in her community to help.

Volunteers included the Coupon Brigade, a group of retired women who came to sort the paper and cardboard. In return they were allowed to keep any coupons they found. They traded them back and forth — a tuna coupon for a margarine coupon, or two cat foods for a tuna. There was always a waiting list for the Coupon Brigade.

John Reindl, an environmental engineer who worked for the university, remembers going to see Milly and Jenny. It was cold inside the warehouse, so Milly was wearing a winter coat and a babushka, a scarf to keep her head warm. Dressed like this, she reminded John of his own mother. Like his mom, Milly had kind eyes, and she was also very smart and practical. For example, Milly and Jenny would be working outside, hauling discarded plastic, and their hands would get raw. If Milly found a bottle of skin lotion, she'd squeeze out whatever was left and use it.

"Milly was like that," he said. "Nothing was to be wasted."

Spreading the Word

Milly and Jenny kept going out and about, educating people and helping nearby towns establish their own recycling programs. It was easier to just throw everything into the garbage, but recycling would save them money. It cost a lot to have garbage trucked out to the landfill.

Milly went to talk to community groups, women's groups, anyone who would let her. She used to walk into meetings carrying big black garbage bags, and as she talked she'd pull out recyclable objects — cans, plastic items, cardboard — to illustrate her points. She'd list the advantages of recycling: saving space in the land-fill so it would last longer, reducing the cost of col-lecting garbage, creating jobs and saving energy and natural resources.

Milly and Jenny went

Milly Zantow

to visit the students at Spruce Street School. The principal made it extra fun by arranging for each kid to have a can of Sun Drop, a popular local soft drink. Once the students drank their pop, they crushed the cans and collected them, and E-Z bought them for recycling. That made it easy for the kids to understand the economic benefits of recycling. Milly and Jenny also explained the ecological benefits.

All of this may seem obvious now, because Milly and people like her worked very hard to make recycling an ordinary part of everyday life. But when she got started, people were only beginning to think about it. Until then, there were only a few cities that had places where you could drop off your recyclables.

In 1968, Madison, Wisconsin, had been one of the first places to set up a system to collect bundles of newspapers at the curb, just like Milly would see done in Japan ten years later. The same year, the aluminum industry in the US began to recycle used aluminum. This was the beginning of a big change around the world.

THE GAR-BARGE

Can you imagine traveling 6,000 miles (9,656 kilometers) looking for a place to dump 3,000 tons of trash? In 1987, the garbage barge *Mobro 4000* was refused at the full landfill in Islip, Long Island, and then again in North Carolina and Louisiana. It kept sailing south and anchored off the coast of Florida after being turned away by the Mexican Navy and the country of Belize.

Eventually the *Mobro* sailed back to New York. It became famous as a symbol of the crisis caused by the lack of landfill space — exactly what had inspired Milly ten years earlier. Before it was unloaded, Greenpeace activists hung a banner on it that said, "Next time ... try recycling."

Milly was contributing to that change. When she and Jenny started E-Z, even people who understood the idea of large-scale recycling of paper and aluminum thought it couldn't be done yet for plastics. They told Milly she was twenty years ahead of her time. But she was confident that she could figure out how to make it work and that she could convince people to do it. In fact, only five years after the head of the Solid Waste Committee of the Sauk County Board told Milly that it "wasn't practical" to recycle plastics, the entire board voted to make a rule that everyone *had* to recycle.

Milly was changing the world by changing people's minds.

Town by Town

As Milly was figuring out how to make plastics recycling succeed and convince other communities to do it too, her work was starting to inspire others. In 1982, some people who had been working with Milly founded a local group called Sauk County Advocates for Resource Conservation and Economy (S.C.A.R.C.E.). They wanted to do more outreach, spreading the word to other towns and cities, but they also wanted to change public policy. That is, they wanted to see rules put in place that would encourage people to recycle.

For example, they were able to convince some towns to charge tipping fees. Imagine a dump truck full of garbage backing up to the landfill. How does it unload? It tips backwards so all the garbage slides out. As soon as it started to cost money to tip each load of garbage,

everybody wanted to dump less so they could pay less. That made recycling more popular.

By working with the members of S.C.A.R.C.E., Milly "multiplied herself" — one person became many. Together they were able to make more positive changes for everyone. In fact, that's the way most changes are made in the world.

Plastics 1 through 7

In late 1982, Milly and Jenny sold E-Z to another recycling company. But Milly was still interested in spreading the idea of recycling.

A company called Midwest Plastics was using E-Z's ground-up plastic to make culverts, drainage pipes and little black wheels for children's toys. But the recycling of plastic was still considered too difficult in most places because there was no easy way to tell the different plastics apart. Not everyone could do the tests that Milly had learned at Boo U. People from near and far contacted Milly and asked her how. She knew that plastics would never be widely recycled until it was easy for everybody to identify the seven types without the dangerous tests.

She and Jenny thought about it. Milly discussed it with her family at the dinner table, considering one idea, then another. They needed a system that anyone could understand, and it would have to be as useful to the plastics companies as to consumers.

"We came up with the idea of a little imprint on the bottom of every container. A

little triangle emblem with a number inserted in it. And that would identify what the plastic was. One, two, three … on up," Milly said.

They talked to a lot of people and organizations, trying to have their system accepted, because they knew it wouldn't work unless it was the same everywhere.

HOW IS PLASTIC RECYCLED?

What happens to the plastics you toss in the recycling bin? As you might guess after reading Milly's story, first they are separated by type — numbers 1 through 7. In some places plastics are separated automatically using infrared light, while others use the low-tech "flotation" process, skimming plastic that floats on water to separate it from the kind that sinks.

Then, probably using a machine much like the one Milly and Jenny bought, the plastic items are shredded or ground up. They are washed clean of any bits of labels or other dirt. Then they are dried and melted down before being formed into pellets with the funny name "nurdles," which are used to make new plastic items.

Finally, in 1988, Milly and other recyclers across the US succeeded in convincing the Society of the Plastics Industry (SPI), an association of plastic producers, to adopt the triangle symbol with its numbers. The triangle symbol had already been in use for a few years by paper recyclers, but the idea of putting the numbers inside it to identify the different plastics really made large-scale plastics recycling possible.

Milly had started a snowball rolling across North America. That year there were only ten plastics recycling plants in all of Canada; only eight years later, there were 105, more than ten times as many. In the US, programs for collecting recyclables at the curb, which is the most convenient and therefore the most successful, jumped from 1,000 in 1988 to 5,000 only four years later. In 1993, Americans recycled over 500,000 tons of plastic, and in 2012, 2.8 *million* tons. That's a lot of landfill space saved — and a lot of petroleum. The SPI estimates that every ton of plastic bottles recycled saves about 3.8 barrels of oil.

One Person Can Lead the Way

From the moment she saw the first bundles of recyclable materials in Japan to ten years later when her numbering system became the international standard, Milly's achievements were impressive. She set up a business, created new markets for objects made out of recycled plastic, saw many communities set up recycling depots, educated the general public about recycling and helped change public policy, multiplying herself as she went.

But Milly didn't stop there. For years afterward, she advised communities on how to set up their own plastics recycling systems, much as she had done for the towns around her home in southern Wisconsin. She talked to government agencies in North America and elsewhere to explain how recycling could work and why it was important. She was even invited to visit Mexico.

Milly played an important role in the creation of Wisconsin's 1989 recycling law, which said it was no longer legal to dump recyclable materials in landfills and required local governments to run recycling programs for plastic, metal, paper, glass and more. The

BIODEGRADABLE PLASTIC

What will we do when there is no new plastic being made? Going back to the materials we used before — wood, metal, paper, glass — is one possibility.

Bioplastics, made from plants like corn or potatoes, is another. These are renewable resources — we can grow more — and some of them can be composted. This eliminates the landfill problem and the garbage problem (although growing corn to make bioplastic ice-cream dishes may not be society's best choice if it means corn for food becomes scarce). But new bioplastics are being developed all the time. For example, a new bioplastic was recently introduced that can be used for 3D printing.

A third answer is to find brand new materials. Some people are experimenting with a substance that, like plastic, makes light, inexpensive furniture that lasts a long time. They are growing this furniture. From mushrooms!

Not the mushrooms we eat, but fungi that create dense, strong networks of roots called mycelia. Plant wastes such as corn stalks are packed into a mold and injected with the fungus. As it digests the corn stalks, it sends out a tough web of roots made of chitin, the hard stuff that makes up the shells of lobsters and insects. The finished chair (or whatever product is being made) is then heated or dried.

first state law requiring recycling in the US had only been passed three years before in Rhode Island. Thanks to the work of Milly Zantow and many of her fellow citizens, Wisconsin had become a national recycling leader. A perfect fit for the state where Earth Day was invented!

When she graduated from high school, Milly won several college scholarships, but she never had a chance to go. Instead her family sent her to Virginia to look after her sister who was recovering from brain surgery. Milly always considered herself an uneducated farm girl, but she made up for any lack of formal schooling with sheer brainpower and determination.

Milly showed people how to challenge the idea that some things aren't recyclable. In fact, John Reindl says he learned from her that *anything* can be recycled if you try hard enough. But her efforts demonstrated a much larger lesson — that you can push past your limits to accomplish something important, and you can push other people too.

Milly never stopped encouraging people to recycle. At the age of ninety-one, living in a nursing home and suffering from a serious illness, she taped several colorful pages of information about recycling on the door of her room so anyone passing by could read them.

No wonder she was described as having "an unstoppable spirit."

Glossary

advocates People who speak in favor of something or someone. You can be an advocate of an idea or advocate for someone who needs your support.

aluminum A light, easily recycled metal often used for soda and beer cans as well as in construction and manufacturing.

babushka A head scarf worn by women, tied under the chin. The word also means "grandmother" in Russian.

bioplastic A substance used for the same purposes as petroleum-based plastic, but usually made from plant materials, such as corn or potato starch. "Bio" comes from the Greek word for life.

brigade An army unit or an organized group of workers.

chitin The material that makes up the hard shells of some insects and creatures like lobsters, and is also produced by some fungi.

compost A rich addition to soil that results from the rotting of plant wastes, such as vegetable peels, and other organic materials. Used to improve soil health and quality.

culvert A pipe that allows water to flow under a road or other barrier.

ecological About the relationships between plants and animals and the natural environment.

economic Relating to the ways money or other forms of value work in society.

infrared A type of radiation invisible to the human eye. Infrared light has slightly longer waves than red light, which has the longest we can see.

landfill A giant hole in the ground that gets filled with garbage. The trash is compacted and layered with earth to take up less space and reduce effects on human health and the environment.

microbeads Tiny beads of plastic used to make toothpaste or other products more effective scrubbers.

mycelia The fine strands that are the growing parts of fungi.

nurdle The basic plastic pellet that is used in manufacturing. Some recycled plastic is formed into nurdles.

ore Rocks that are very rich in metals and other minerals.

PET (polyethylene terephthalate) The most commonly used plastic resin (#1). First used by the military during World War II, it quickly became a popular material in consumer goods.

petroleum The basic form of oil found in the earth. It is processed into many products, including gasoline, other fuels and plastic. The word "petroleum" comes from two Latin words — "petra," which means "rock," and "oleum," which means "oil."

plastic Any of several substances made from petroleum and used for a wide variety of purposes. The word "plastic," like its ancient Greek ancestor, means easy to shape.

public policy Guidelines created with the help of experts so government decision-makers have the information they need. Public policy is often used to encourage desired actions.

refining Taking impurities out of a substance. In the case of petroleum it means processing crude oil to make it into products such as gasoline, oils and other fuels.

renewable Replaceable through a natural process. For example, trees and other plants are renewable resources because we can grow more.

warp The long fibers that are attached to a loom. Other fibers (the weft or woof) are woven in and out of them to create the finished rug or cloth.

The seven types of plastics (plastic resins) and some things they are commonly used for.

△1	PET	*Polyethylene terephthalate* Water and soft drink bottles, fleece clothing, blankets/throws, boat sails.
△2	HDPE	*High-density polyethylene* Milk and laundry soap jugs, pill bottles, lightweight grocery bags, plastic lumber, folding chairs, plumbing pipes, building insulation.
△3	V	*Polyvinyl chloride* Sewer and water pipes, electrical cable insulation, shower curtains, credit cards, clothes, shoes.
△4	LDPE	*Low-density polyethylene* Heavy plastic shopping bags, plastic wrap, juice boxes, playground equipment.
△5	PP	*Polypropylene* Food containers, medical and laboratory items, clear plastic bags, carpets, lightweight rope, diapers.
△6	PS	*Polystyrene* Disposable plastic forks and spoons, DVD jewel cases, Styrofoam.
△7	(Other)	*Other* Acrylic and nylon fabrics, bioplastics.

For Further Reading

Compost: A Family Guide to Making Soil from Scraps by Ben Raskin. Roost Books, 2014.

Gaylord Nelson: Champion for Our Earth by Sheila Terman Cohen. Wisconsin Historical Society Press, 2013.

Here Comes the Garbage Barge! by Jonah Winter and Red Nose Studio. Penguin Random House, 2010.

Heroes of the Environment: True Stories of People Who Are Helping to Protect Our Planet by Harriet Rohmer, illustrated by Julie Mc-Laughlin. Chronicle Books, 2009.

Nobody Particular: One Woman's Fight to Save the Bays by Molly Bang. Henry Holt & Company, 2001.

Planting the Trees of Kenya: The Story of Wangari Maathai by Claire A. Nivola. Farrar, Straus & Giroux, 2008.

Plastic, Ahoy! Investigating the Great Pacific Garbage Patch by Patricia Newman, illustrated by Annie Crawley. Millbrook Press, 2014.

Who Was Rachel Carson? by Sarah Fabiny, illustrated by Dede Putra and Nancy Harrison. Grosset & Dunlap, 2014.

Selected Sources

(The videos and websites listed on page 46 may be of interest to young readers.)

Information about Milly Zantow's life came from conversations with her sons Todd Zantow and Jim Stevens and from "Memories of Mildred Louise Taylor Stevens Zantow, 1923-2014," a short account of Milly's past that she wrote for her family in 2009, when she was eighty-six years old. Her daughter-in-law Cheryl Zantow put all the handwritten pieces in chronological order, edited them and made copies at the time of Milly's death in 2014. Elizabeth (Liz) Nevers and John Reindl also offered invaluable information about Milly's recycling career.

Books and Periodicals

Melosi, Martin V. *Garbage in the Cities: Refuse, Reform, and the Environment*, Revised Edition. University of Pittsburgh Press, 2005.
Archives of the *Sauk Prairie Star*, available at the Sauk City Public Library.

Videos

"Plastics One through Seven: A Short Film about an Extraordinary Woman." Video interview with Milly Zantow and Jenny Ehl by Liese Dart.
www.youtube.com/watch?v=AM6-NqmzI1I
"Voyage of the *Mobro*." Video about the famous garbage barge.
www.nytimes.com/video/booming/100000002206073/voyage-of-the-mobro-4000.html

Websites

Canadian Plastics Industry Association
Includes information on recycling plastics, teachers' tools, games and activities.
www.plastics.ca/EducationalTools/GamesActivities/index.php
Environment and Climate Change Canada
"Youth Zone" activities and resources for kids.
http://ec.gc.ca/sce-cew/default.asp?lang=En&n=87740C94-1
International Crane Foundation
Includes activity packs and other resources for teachers and classrooms.
www.savingcranes.org

The *Plastiki*
All about the boat made from recycled garbage.
http://theplastiki.com
Society of the Plastics Industry
Recycling page provides a wide range of information.
www.plasticsindustry.org/Recycling/content.cfm?ItemNumber=1271&navItemNumber=12122
United States Environmental Protection Agency
"Recycle City" game, activities for kids and resources for teachers.
www3.epa.gov/recyclecity/activity.htm
Wisconsin Department of Natural Resources
"Recycling and Beyond" information, games and activities on recycling and reusing trash.
http://dnr.wi.gov/org/caer/ce/eek/earth/recycle

Source Notes

8 Milly's grandma ... stories. "Memories of Mildred Louise Taylor Stevens Zantow, 1923-2014."
14 "garbage crisis." Martin V. Melosi, *Garbage in the Cities: Refuse, Reform, and the Environment*, Revised Edition (Pittsburgh: University of Pittsburgh Press, 2005), p. 190.
19 What did they do ... asked. "Plastics One through Seven: A Short Film about an Extraordinary Woman," YouTube video, 8:26, a documentary film by Liese Dart, October 30, 2012, posted by University of Wisconsin Extension, www.youtube.com/watch?v=AM6-NqmzI1I.
21 "just died laughing when they saw us." Ibid.
21 "It weighed a ton!" Ibid.
22 "Waste isn't waste until it's wasted." *Baraboo News Republic*, March 6, 2010.
22 "It's a sin to bury money." *Sauk Prairie Star*, May 15, 1980.
22 "heartsick." *Sauk Prairie Star*, January 24, 1980.
25 "You have ... people." Liz Nevers interview, September 5, 2014.

25 Milly laughed when, years ... school. Milly Zantow interview, May 14, 2014.

26-27 "We hope ... natural resources." *Sauk Prairie Star*, May 29, 1980.

29 "And then ... it blew away." YouTube video, "Plastics One through Seven."

31 "Milly...wasted." John Reindl interview, February 11, 2015.

33 "Next time...recycling." www.nytimes.com/video/ booming/100000002206073/voyage-of-the-mobro-4000.html.

34 "wasn't practical." Liz Nevers interview, September 5, 2014.

36 "multiplied herself." Liz Nevers interview, September 5, 2014.

37-38 "We came up with...on up." YouTube video, "Plastics One through Seven."

42 Milly always ... determination. Todd Zantow and Jim Stevens interview, June 19, 2015.

42 "In fact ... people too." John Reindl interview, February 11, 2015.

43 "an unstoppable spirit." Ibid.

45 Plastics identification code. www.plasticsindustry. org/AboutPlastics/content.cfm?ItemNumber =823

Acknowledgments

Many, many people helped make this book possible. The seed was planted during an event organized by the local citizen environmentalists of Sauk Area Climate Awareness and Action. I thank them for that and for all their work. I am also grateful to Liese Dart, whose video of Milly, "Plastics One through Seven," was tremendously helpful. We are lucky to have this wonderful record of Milly telling her own story.

Liz Nevers and John Reindl enthusiastically shared their knowledge and experiences of Milly and helped me understand the larger context of her achievements. Two of Milly's sons, Todd Zantow and Jim Stevens, also kindly shared information about their extraordinary mother. The co-founder of the International Crane Foundation (ICF), George Archibald, gave me an hour of his time, as well as a tour of his garden and a dahlia as big as my head. Claire Mirande helped me track down information I needed at ICF on more than one occasion with characteristic warmth and generosity.

Young readers Graham Doyle, Isabel MacDonald-Palmer, Lora MacDonald-Palmer and Lucie Markus and grownup reader, writer and weaver Alice Zorn all significantly improved the book with their thoughtful and sophisticated feedback.

My editor Nan Froman and publisher Sheila Barry were essential guides through a book-creation process that was very different from anything I'd ever done before. I am indebted to them for their skill, patience, good humor and professionalism — all as I have come to expect from Groundwood Books. Thanks also to illustrator Scot Ritchie for adding visual charm.

I am deeply grateful for the support, moral and practical, of Fred Lauing, my dear love.

I was fortunate to meet Milly several months before her death in 2014. She and her husband Woody (Forrest Zantow) welcomed me and Fred warmly. Although she was ill and we couldn't speak for long, Milly's grace and openness made a permanent impression on me.

Index